Boc

IN RECITAL®

Throughout the Year
(with Performance Strategies)
Volume Two

ABOUT THE SERIES • A NOTE TO THE TEACHER

In Recital® — Throughout the Year is a series that focuses on fabulous repertoire, intended to motivate your students. We know that to motivate, the teacher must challenge the student with attainable goals. This series makes that possible. The fine composers and arrangers of this series have created musically engaging pieces, which have been carefully leveled and address the technical strengths and weaknesses of students. The wide range of styles in each book of the series complements other FJH publications and will help you to plan students' recital repertoire for the entire year. You will find original solos and duets that focus on different musical and technical issues, giving you the selection needed to accommodate your students' needs. There are arrangements of famous classical themes, as well as repertoire written for Halloween, Christmas, and Fourth of July recitals. In this way, your student will have recital pieces throughout the entire year! Additionally, the series provides a progressive discussion on the art of performance. The earlier levels offer tips on recital preparation, while the later levels address more advanced technical and psychological issues that help to realize successful performances.

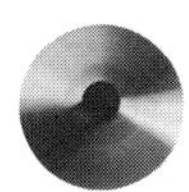

Use the enclosed CD as a teaching and motivational tool. Have your students listen to the recording and discuss interpretation with you!

Production: Frank and Gail Hackinson
Production Coordinators: Philip Groeber and Isabel Otero Bowen
Cover: Terpstra Design, San Francisco
Cover Piano Illustration: Keith Criss
Engraving: Kevin Olson and Tempo Music Press, Inc.
Printer: Tempo Music Press, Inc.

ISBN-13: 978-1-56939-476-2

9 Recital Preparation Tips • For the Teacher

1. Consider a tiered approach to developing comfort in performance. Make "mini" performances a regular occurrence, probably without even calling them performances. Have a student play for the student who follows his/her lesson. It doesn't matter if their leveling is different; the older students are naturally nice to the young and the young provide a non-threatening audience for the older. Have students play mini concerts at home. Younger students may enjoy concerts for their favorite stuffed animals each day after practice. Advise older students to practice performing by recording themselves. Of course, you will tailor these suggestions according to each student's personality. Just remember, *no venue is too small and frequency is the key*. Suggestions for mini-performances and performance strategies are also addressed on pages 16, 17, and 21.

   Once students are comfortable with these "mini" performances, teachers must create opportunities for students to play in public, so that they will get used to the idea of getting up on stage and playing for others. Studio group lessons or performance classes are perfect for trial performances, then take it to the next step and invite family or friends to a performance class.

   Try these different performance venues and you will be pleased with the results. The "tiered" approach helps performance to become a natural part of piano study.

2. Make sure that your students have the opportunity to perform pieces well within their technical range. These performances will help build student confidence and will make a huge difference when they are playing more challenging repertoire.

3. Have students practice concentrating on the tempo, mood, and dynamics of the piece before beginning to play.

4. Coach students on how to walk purposefully *to* the piano, adjust the bench, and check their position relative to the piano. Have them practice this a lot in the lesson and at home. Familiarity with the process really helps.

5. Talk to your students about how to finish the piece. Coach them to stay with the music until the piece is over. Discuss how they will move at the end of the piece: i.e., quickly moving the hands away from the keyboard, or slowly lifting the hands with the lifting of the pedal, depending on the repertoire.

6. Coach students how to bow and walk purposefully *away* from the piano. Again, practice this together often so that it feels natural to them.

7. Remind students to keep the recital in perspective. The recital piece should be one of several the student is working on, so that they understand that there is "life after the recital."

8. If possible, have a practice session in the performance location. Encourage your students to focus on what they can control and remind them that although a piano may feel differently, their technique will not "go away."

9. Have your students listen to the companion CD. Not only does this give them ideas on how to interpret the pieces, it builds an intuitive knowledge of how the pieces sound, which helps increase confidence and comfort.

The goal is to instill in our students the excitement of playing for others and to demystify the process. There is nothing quite like communicating a piece of music to an audience and then enjoying their positive reaction to it. With our help, our students can perform up to their potential in public and enjoy this exciting and rewarding experience.

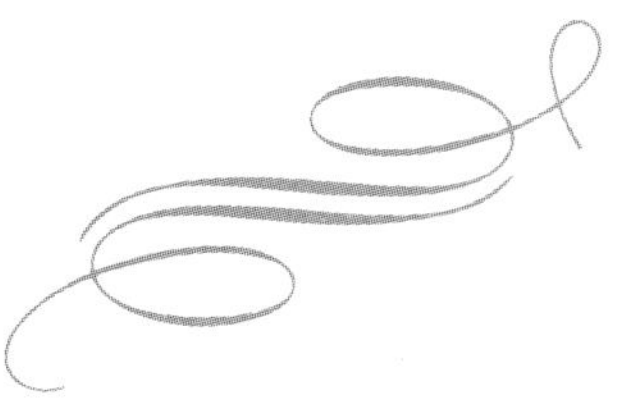

Organization of the Series
In Recital® • Throughout the Year

In Recital® — Throughout the Year is carefully leveled into the following six categories: Early Elementary, Elementary, Late Elementary, Early Intermediate, Intermediate, and Late Intermediate. Each of the works has been selected for its artistic as well as its pedagogical merit.

Book Three — Late Elementary, reinforces the following concepts:

- Eighth notes are added to the basic notes students played in books 1 and 2. Simple triplet patterns as well as the dotted quarter note are introduced at the end of the book.
- Students play different articulations such as *legato* and *staccato* at the same time.
- Students play pieces in a variety of different moods, tempos, and forms.
- Students play blocked and broken major, minor, and diminished chords.
- Pieces reinforce five-finger scales, as well as scale patterns that extend from the usual five-finger patterns (with finger crossings).
- Blocked intervals up to a sixth, double thirds, and hand-over hand arpeggios are played.
- Students continue to experience movement up and down the keyboard, and the use of the pedal is continued and expanded to create a big sound as well as to play artistically.
- Pieces continue to reinforce basic musical terminology and symbols such as *crescendo*, *decrescendo*, *ritardando*, *fermata*, *mezzo forte*, *mezzo piano*, *forte*, *piano*, *fortissimo*, *pianissimo*, and *D.S.* 𝄋 *al Coda*.
- Keys of C major, G major, F major, A minor, and D minor.

Most of the pieces in Book Three are solos. *Caveman Rock* was composed as an equal part duet. One of the solos has an optional teacher accompaniment to enhance the overall sound of the piece.

Table of Contents

Water Lilies

Valerie Roth Roubos

17
mp
21
mf
25
mp
rit.
29
a tempo
8va
p
rit.

Dance of the Gnomes

Kevin Costley

17 **Slower, with suspense**

mp

21 *8va both hands*

mp

rit.

25 **Tempo I**

mf

29

molto rit.

cautiously

32

a tempo

f

Imanuel

Caveman Rock
Secondo

Kevin Olson

Heavily, in two (𝅗𝅥 = 92-100)

Play both hands one octave lower throughout

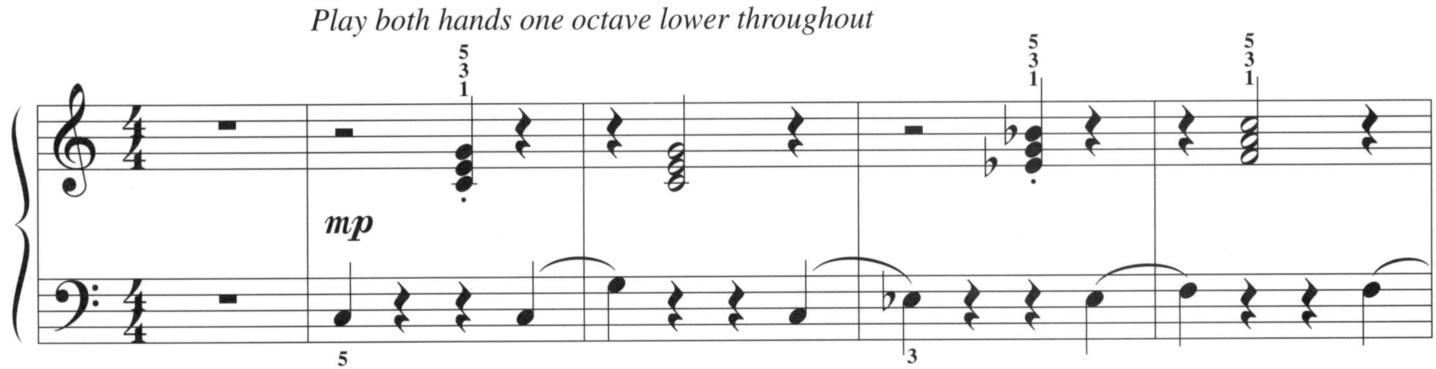

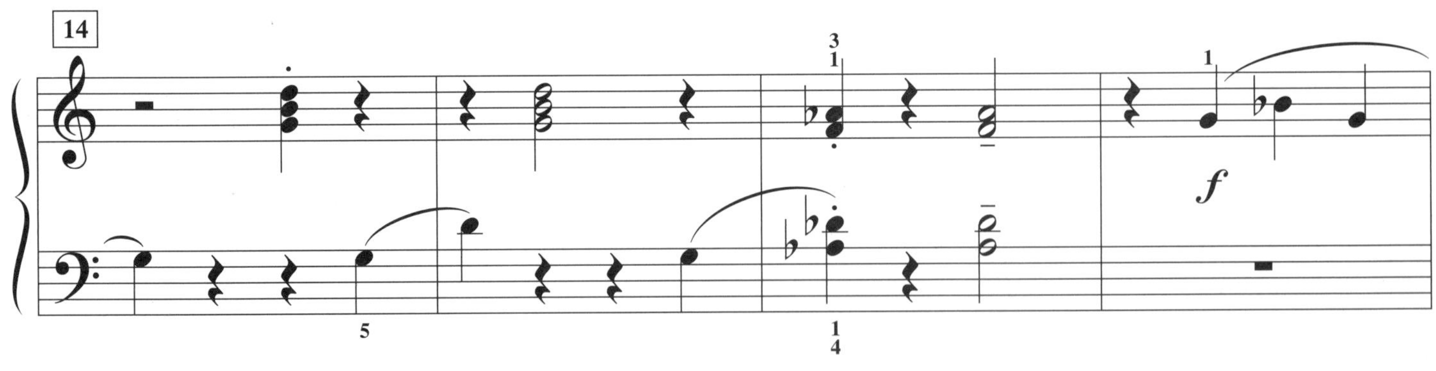

Caveman Rock
Primo

Kevin Olson

Heavily, in two (𝅗𝅥 = 92-100)

Play both hands one octave higher throughout

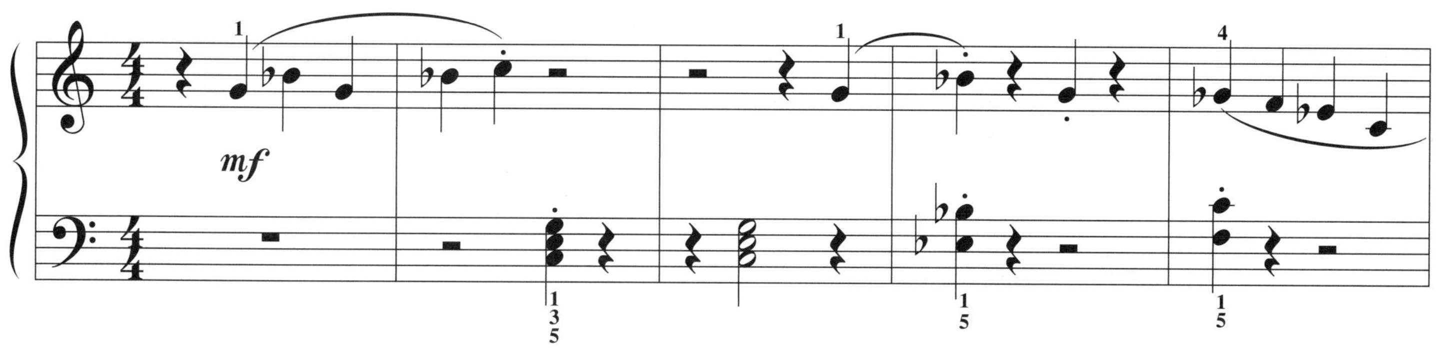

Secondo

18
22
26
mf
f
30
mf
Optional: tremolo on all of the notes for a big finish!
34
mp
molto rit.
f sub.
(1 - 2 - 3 - 4)
ff

Primo

18
mf
22
26
mf
f
30
mf
34
mp
molto rit.
f sub.
ff
Optional: tremolo on all of the notes for a big finish!

Pavane pour une infante défunte

Maurice Ravel
arr. Timothy Brown

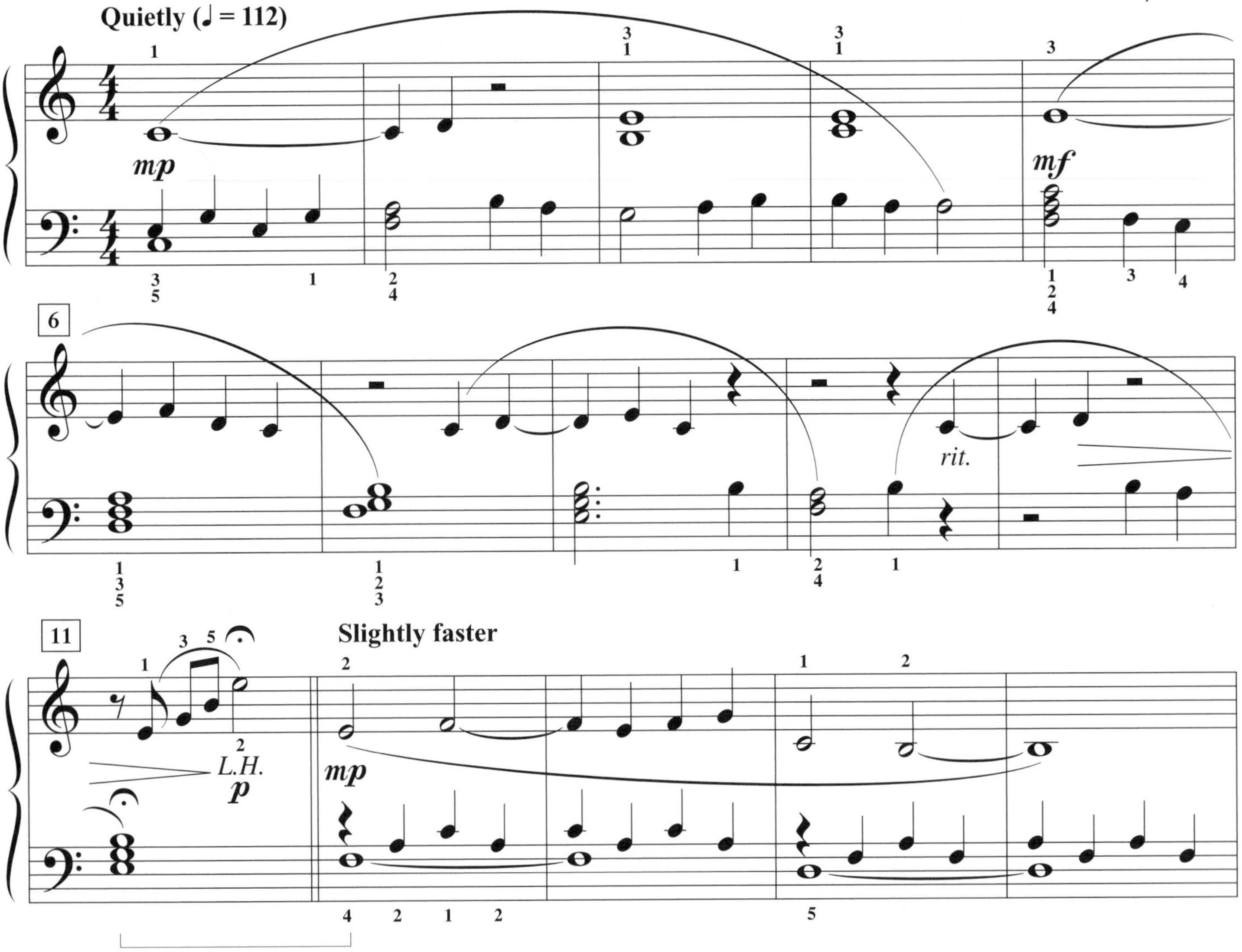

Quietly (♩ = 112)
mp
mf
6
rit.
11
L.H.
p
Slightly faster
mp

Teacher Accompaniment: (*Student plays one octave higher*)

2
26
p
mp
6
8
32
To Coda
rit.
11
pp
Slightly faster
p
ped. simile

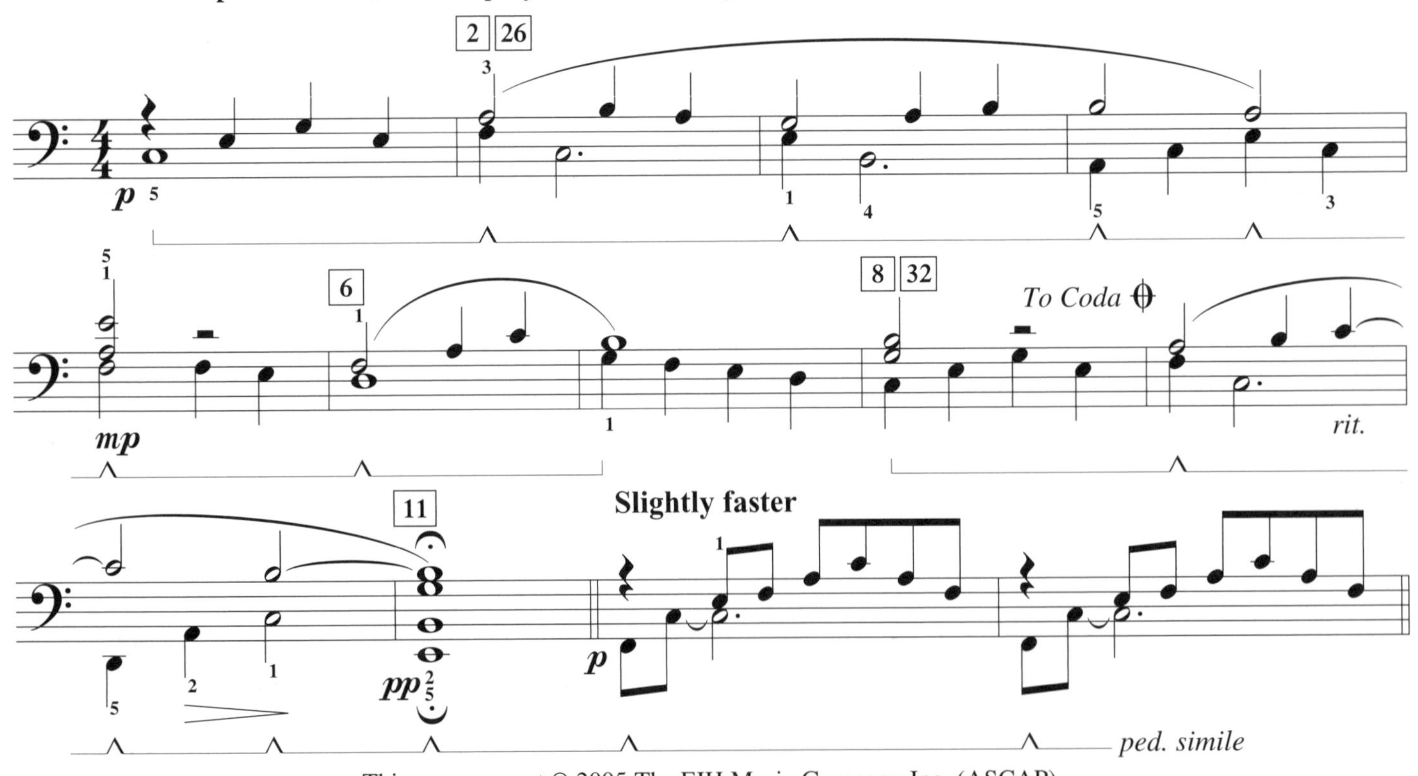

16
21
a tempo
rit.
26
32
rit.
14 16
21
D.C. al Coda
Coda
rit.
rit.

A Note to Students

Welcome to the wonderful world of performing. Performing in public is a special skill that can be learned, just like learning how to swim! It might seem a bit scary at first, but once you learn this skill, performing can be a whole lot of fun!

Here are two keys to successful and enjoyable performances:

- Prepare well beforehand
- Practice performing in front of others

Preparation:
Here is a list of things to do to make sure you know your piece extremely well:
(Place a check in the box for each day you complete the task and start four weeks before the recital.)

4 weeks	*3 weeks*	*2 weeks*	*1 week*	
				Can you play the entire piece, hands alone, *from memory?* (Listening to each individual part helps you to be completely aware of what each hand is playing.)
				Can you sing or hum the melody away from the piano?
				Can you start your piece at four *different* places in the music? (You and your teacher can mark with a star ☆ four good starting places).
				Can you play the piece from beginning to end at "half tempo"? ("Half tempo" means to play it with all of the correct rhythms, notes, and dynamics, but at half of the speed you would play it when performing it.)
				After playing the piece, ask yourself: Did it sound like the title suggests? Did I bring the piece to life?
				Listen to the recording of your recital piece for ideas on how to play it. You can mark directly in your score what you hear.

Starting four weeks before your actual performance, practice these strategies every day. It might be difficult to do all of these at first, but the more you practice, the easier they will become. Remember, if you prepare well, the performance day will be easy and fun!

You can use this page as a practice guide for every recital piece you play in this book!

Two weeks before your recital, try these two performance tips:

1. Every *other* day, play your piece through three times in a row, without stopping. Pretend you are playing in the recital. If you make a little mistake, just keep going. This practice strategy helps you to learn how you will feel when you are performing your piece(s) in a recital, in front of an audience.

2 weeks... 2 tips...

• play your piece through three times in a row...

pretend you are playing in the recital...

• play in front of an audience...

if you make a little mistake, just keep going...

Then, *after* the three performances, think about the following questions and answer them below:

Did I play my pieces steadily, making sure that they were rhythmically accurate? (Could I easily hear every single note in the pieces? Was everything clear?) If not, what could I have done better?

____

Did I play my pieces beautifully, with a good sound at every moment? If not, what could I have done better?

____

Did I play the *forte* sections really *forte* and the *piano* sections really *piano*?

____

Was I nervous? Excited? Happy with what I could play?

____

(Your teacher will give you some great input on this question and your answer!)

2. Make arrangements to play in front of an audience. (Your teacher will help you with this!) Part of the fun of learning how to play the piano is to share the music with others!

   Write below the places where you performed your piece(s). After the place, describe the audience's reaction to your playing (they clapped, they smiled, etc.)

   ____

   ____

   ____

To learn the **Steps for a Winning Performance**, turn to page 21.

No Bones About It!

Melody Bober

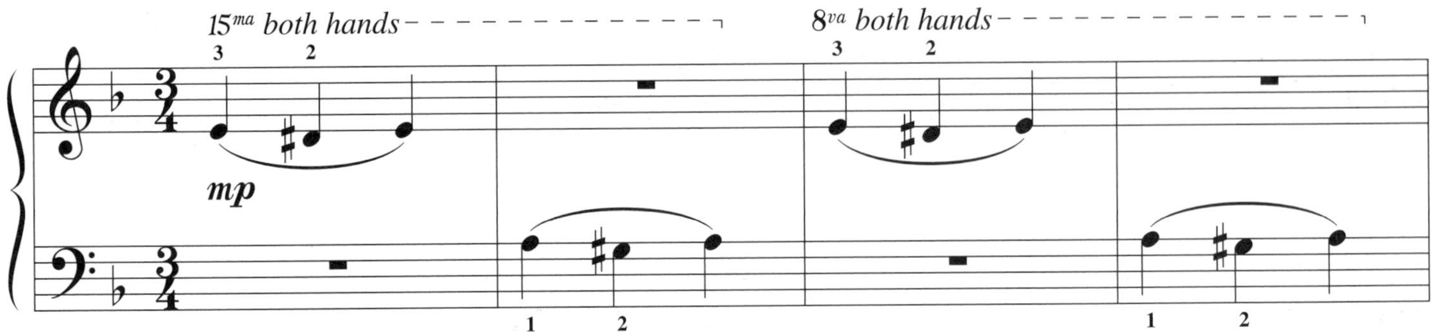

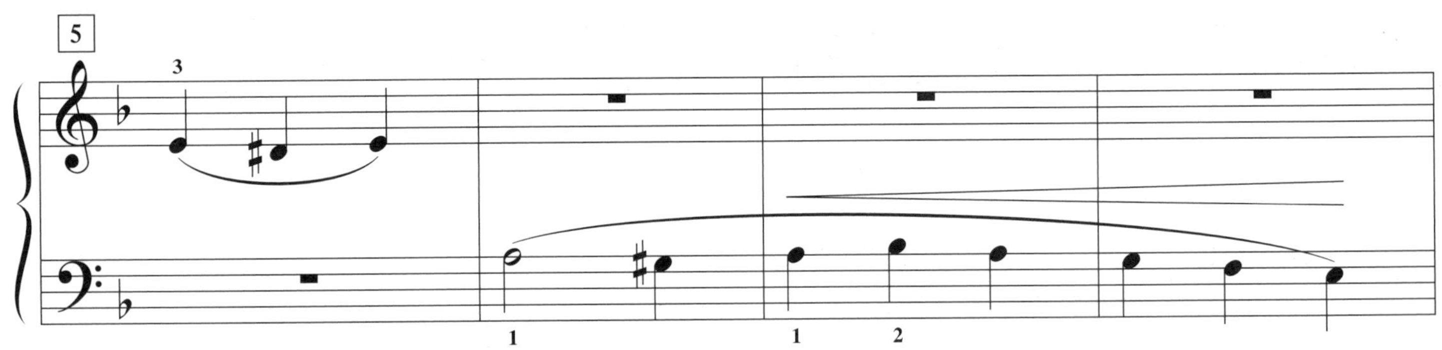

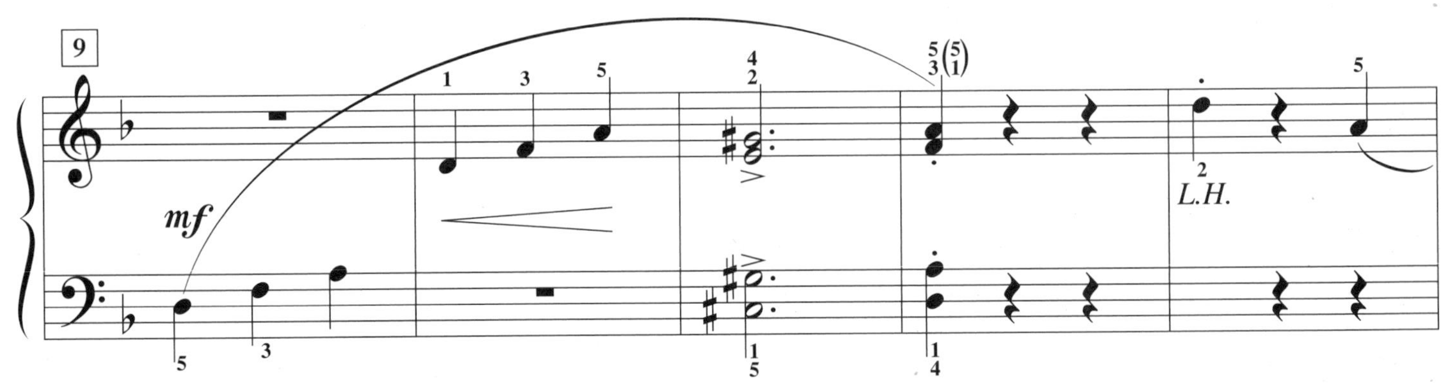

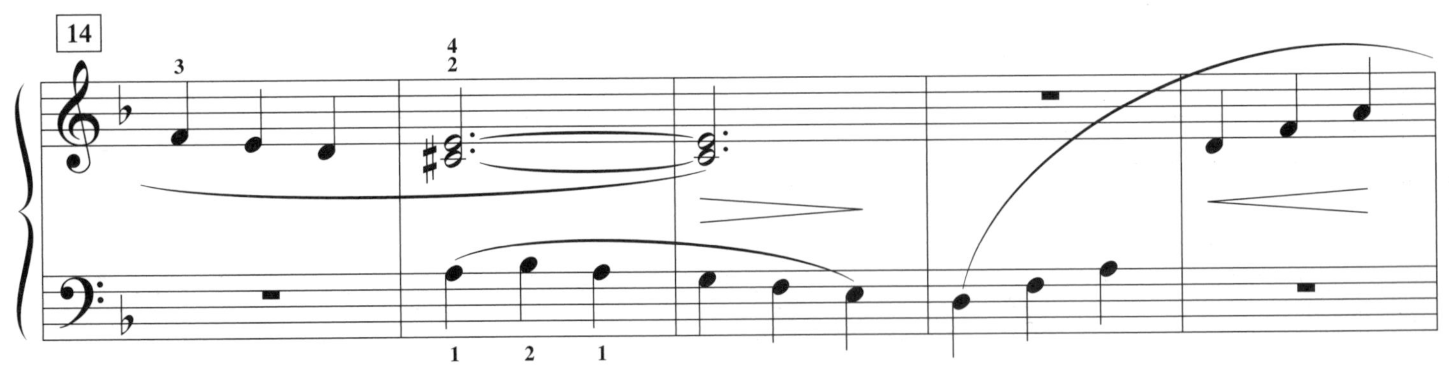

19
L.H.
24
f
mp
29
34
39
8va both hands

43
mf
48
L.H.
53
L.H.
59
p
cresc.
8va both hands
64
8va both hands
mf
p
8va

Practice:

1. Walking to the piano with confidence and with purpose.

2. Standing in front of the piano bench, nodding your head, and smiling at the audience.

3. Sitting at the bench and making sure you are seated at the proper height as well as distance from the keyboard.

4. Thinking about the speed, mood, and dynamics of the piece; and breathing before you begin.

5. Taking your time before you begin. This adds drama and excitement to your performance, and helps you to completely focus.

6. Staying with the music while you play! This means that you think about the notes, dynamics, and phrasing as you play, you feel the emotion of the music, and listen to yourself every single moment.

7. Listening to yourself produce a beautiful sound at all times!

8. Placing your hands in your lap after you finish playing. Remember to bow. It is a way to say "Thank you" to your audience for listening.

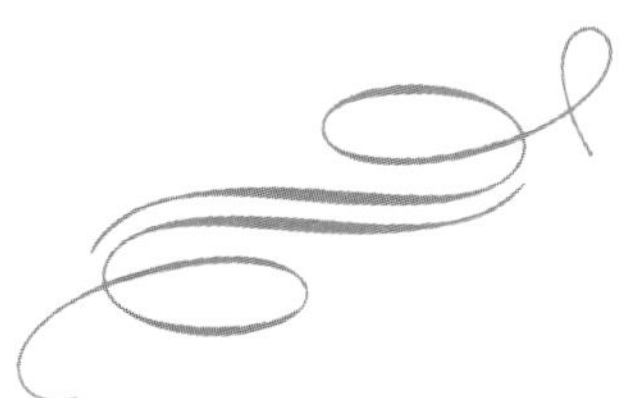

I Saw Three Ships

Traditional English Carol
arr. Elizabeth W. Greenleaf

25
saw three ships come sail - ing in, On Christ - mas
30
Day, on Christ - mas Day; I saw three ships come
35
sail - ing in, On Christ - mas Day in the morn -
40
ing.
cresc.
45
f
rit.

Winter Waltz

Judith R. Strickland

19
23
p
27
31
8va
pp

Theme from Symphony No. 1

Op. 68, Fourth Movement

Johannes Brahms
arr. Edwin McLean

cresc.
mp
f
tr
8va

An American Tapestry

Timothy Brown

17
21
25
29
rallentando
33
a tempo
8va

for Lauren Jankoviak

Clear Sailing

Mary Leaf

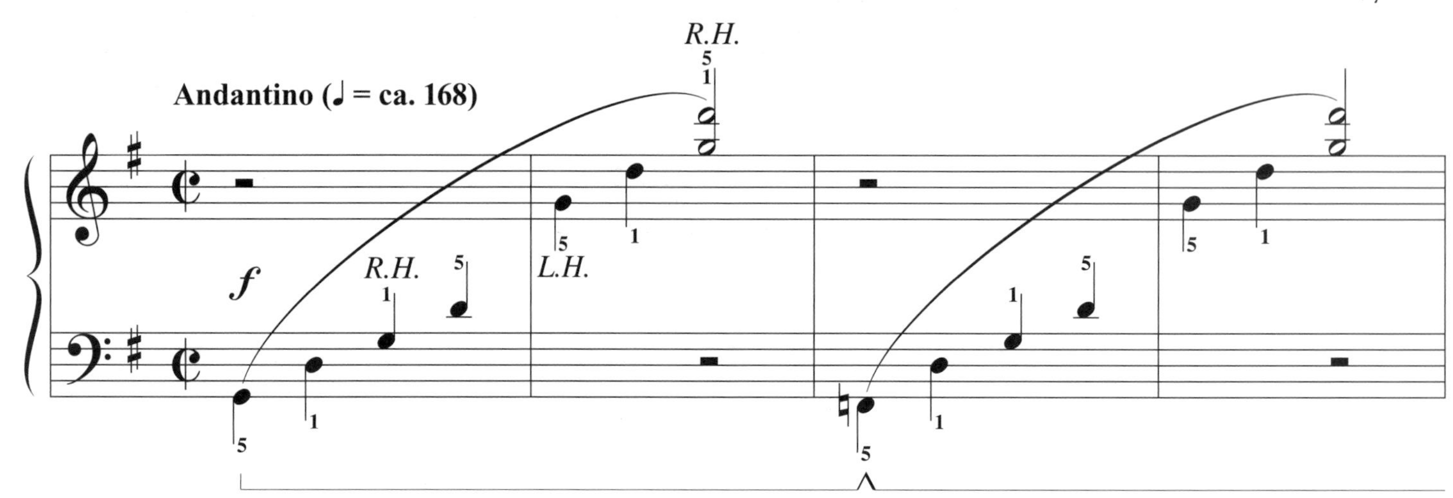

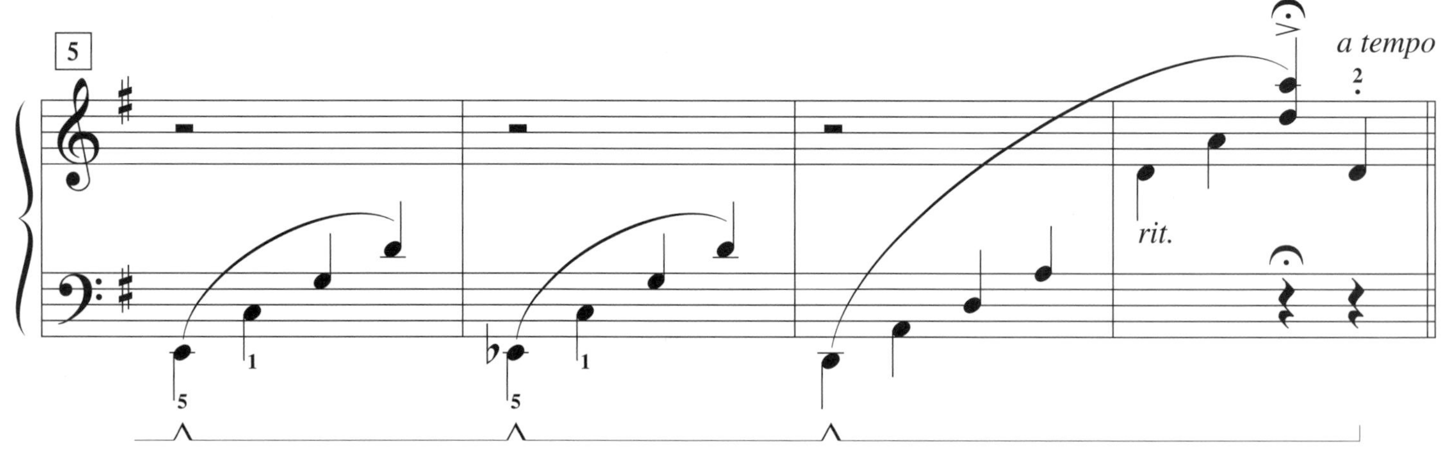

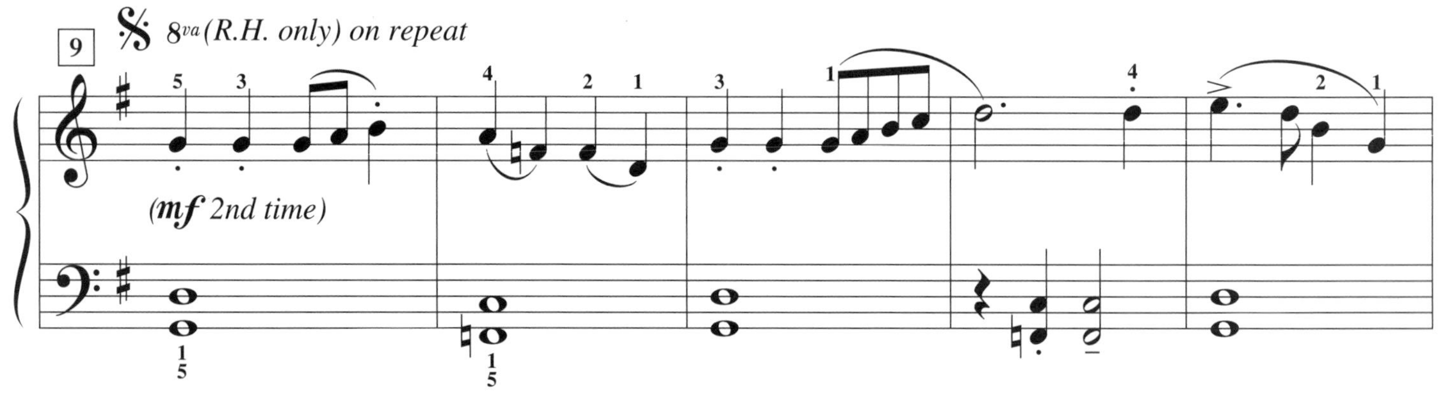

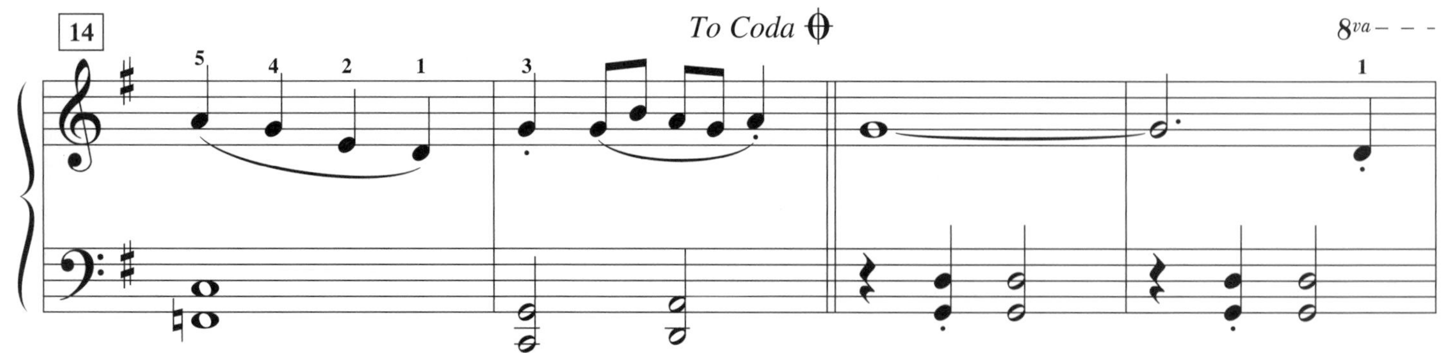

18
(8va)
mp
mf
23
28
33
D.S. al Coda
f
Coda
loco
ff
no rit.
L.H.
8va

About the Composers/Arrangers

Melody Bober

Piano instructor, music teacher, composer, clinician—Melody Bober has been active in music education for over 25 years. As a composer, her goal is to create exciting and challenging pieces that are strong teaching tools to promote a lifelong love, understanding, and appreciation for music. Pedagogy, ear training, and musical expression are fundamentals of Melody's teaching, as well as fostering composition skills in her students.

Melody graduated with highest honors from the University of Illinois with a degree in music education, and later received a master's degree in piano performance. She maintains a large private studio, performs in numerous regional events, and conducts workshops across the country. She and her husband Jeff reside in Minnesota.

Timothy Brown

Timothy Brown holds a master's degree in piano performance from the University of North Texas, where he studied piano with Adam Wodnicki and music composition with Newel Kay Brown. He was later a recipient of a research fellowship from the Royal Holloway, University of London, where he performed postgraduate studies in music composition and orchestration, studying with English composer Brian Lock. His numerous credits as a composer include first prize at the Aliénor International Harpsichord Competition for his harpsichord solo *Suite Española* (Centaur Records). Mr. Brown leads a very active career as an exclusive composer and clinician for The FJH Music Company Inc.

Mr. Brown's works have been performed by concert artist Elaine Funaro on NPR, and most recently at the Spoleto Music Festival and the Library of Congress Concert Series in Washington, D.C. His numerous commissions include a commission by *Clavier* Magazine for his piano solo *Once Upon a Time*, edited by Denes Agay. Mr. Brown is currently a fine arts specialist for the Dallas Public Schools and serves on the advisory board of the Booker T. Washington High School for the Performing and Visual Arts in Dallas, Texas.

Kevin Costley

Kevin Costley holds several graduate degrees in the areas of elementary education and piano pedagogy, and literature, including a doctorate from Kansas State University. For nearly two decades, he was owner and director of The Keyboard Academy, specializing in innovative small group instruction. Kevin served for several years as head of the music department and on the keyboard faculty of Messenger College in Joplin, Missouri.

Kevin is a standing faculty member of Inspiration Point Fine Arts Colony piano and string camp, where he performs and teaches private piano, ensemble classes, and composition. He conducts child development seminars, writes for national publications, serves as a clinician for piano workshops, and adjudicates numerous piano festivals and competitions.

Elizabeth W. Greenleaf

Elizabeth W. Greenleaf received a Piano Teaching Certificate and a Bachelor of Music degree in composition from Florida State University, and a Master of Music degree in piano performance from Louisiana State University.

Elizabeth has been active as a composer, performer, and teacher for over twenty-five years. She has performed many recitals, both as an accompanist for instrumentalists and singers, and as a chamber music player. Her students have ranged from preschoolers to senior citizens, and she has taught at all levels from beginning to advanced. Recently retired from teaching, Elizabeth enjoys composing to meet the needs of students. Her music has received high praise from top teachers throughout the country.

Mary Leaf

Mary Leaf is an independent piano teacher specializing in early elementary through intermediate level students. She enjoys writing music that is descriptive, expressive, imaginative, and fun, while still being musically sound.

Mary received a music education degree from the University of Washington and has done continuing education in pedagogy at North Dakota State University. She has composed and arranged music for a family recorder ensemble, and has been active as a performer, accompanist, handbell ringer, and choir member at her church. She is also active in area contests as an accompanist. Mary and her husband Ron have five children and live in Bismarck, North Dakota.

Edwin McLean

Edwin McLean is a composer living in Chapel Hill, North Carolina. He is a graduate of the Yale School of Music, where he studied with Krzysztof Penderecki and Jacob Druckman. He also holds a master's degree in music theory and a bachelor's degree in piano performance from the University of Colorado.

Mr. McLean has authored over 200 publications for The FJH Music Company, ranging from *The FJH Classic Music Dictionary* to original works for pianists from beginner to advanced. His highly-acclaimed works for harpsichord have been performed internationally and are available on the Miami Bach Society recording, *Edwin McLean: Sonatas for 1, 2, and 3 Harpsichords*. His 2011 solo jazz piano album Don't Say Goodbye (CD1043) includes many of his advanced works for piano published by FJH.

Edwin McLean began his career as a professional arranger. Currently, he is senior editor for The FJH Music Company Inc.

Kevin Olson

Kevin Olson is an active pianist, composer, and member of the piano faculty at Utah State University, where he teaches piano literature, pedagogy, and accompanying courses. In addition to his collegiate teaching responsibilities, Kevin directs the Utah State Youth Conservatory, which provides weekly group and private piano instruction to more than 200 pre-college community students. The National Association of Schools of Music has recently recognized the Conservatory as a model for pre-college piano instruction programs. Before teaching at Utah State, he was on the faculty at Elmhurst College near Chicago and Humboldt State University in northern California.

A native of Utah, Kevin began composing at age five. When he was twelve, his composition, *An American Trainride,* received the Overall First Prize at the 1983 National PTA Convention at Albuquerque, New Mexico. Since then he has been a Composer in Residence at the National Conference on Keyboard Pedagogy, and has written music commissioned and performed by groups such as the American Piano Quartet, Chicago a cappella, the Rich Matteson Jazz Festival, MTNA (Music Teachers National Association), and several piano teacher associations around the country. Kevin maintains a large piano studio, teaching students of a variety of ages and abilities. Many of the needs of his own piano students have inspired more than 100 books and solos published by The FJH Music Company Inc., which he joined as a writer in 1994.

Valerie Roth Roubos

Valerie Roth Roubos earned degrees in music theory, composition, and flute performance from the University of Wyoming. Ms. Roubos maintains a studio in her home in Spokane, Washington, where she teaches flute, piano, and composition. Active as a performer, adjudicator, lecturer, and accompanist, Ms. Roubos has lectured and taught master classes at the Washington State Music Teachers Conference, Holy Names Music Camp, and the Spokane and Tri-Cities chapters of Washington State Music Teachers Association. She has played an active role in the Spokane Music Teachers Association and WSMTA.

In 2001, the South Dakota Music Teachers Association selected Ms. Roubos as Composer of the Year, and with MTNA commissioned her to write *An American Portrait: Scenes from the Great Plains,* published by The FJH Music Company Inc. Ms. Roubos was chosen to be the 2004–2005 composer-in-residence at Washington State University. In 2006, WSMTA selected her as Composer of the Year.

Judith R. Strickland

Judith R. Strickland received a bachelor's degree in music from Mary Baldwin College in Staunton, Virginia, and a master's degree in sacred music from Union Theological Seminary in New York. In addition to actively teaching both piano and organ, Judith also serves as accompanist for the Community Chorus and Piedmont Choral Society, as well as for numerous instrumental and vocal soloists.

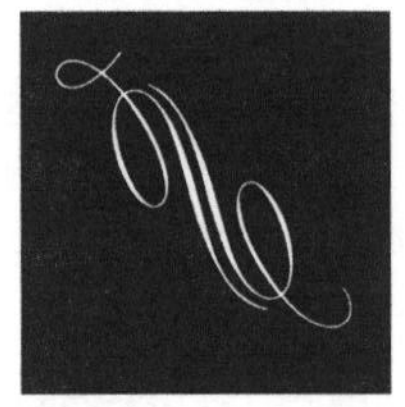